1 MONTH OF FREE READING

at

www.ForgottenBooks.com

By purchasing this book you are eligible for one month membership to ForgottenBooks.com, giving you unlimited access to our entire collection of over 1,000,000 titles via our web site and mobile apps.

To claim your free month visit:
www.forgottenbooks.com/free586551

* Offer is valid for 45 days from date of purchase. Terms and conditions apply.

ISBN 978-0-484-59842-2
PIBN 10586551

This book is a reproduction of an important historical work. Forgotten Books uses state-of-the-art technology to digitally reconstruct the work, preserving the original format whilst repairing imperfections present in the aged copy. In rare cases, an imperfection in the original, such as a blemish or missing page, may be replicated in our edition. We do, however, repair the vast majority of imperfections successfully; any imperfections that remain are intentionally left to preserve the state of such historical works.

Forgotten Books is a registered trademark of FB &c Ltd.
Copyright © 2018 FB &c Ltd.
FB &c Ltd, Dalton House, 60 Windsor Avenue, London, SW19 2RR.
Company number 08720141. Registered in England and Wales.

For support please visit www.forgottenbooks.com

PREFACE.

In the opinion of many there in nothing determinate in punctuation : punctuate as you like, they say, and you have authority for it. That writers differ in their styles of pointing, and even that many writers are glaringly inconsistent in using the marks of punctuation, is well known to every observant reader ; but it is not the case that there are no fixed principles to govern the art.

Punctuation, like rhetoric, grammar, or orthoëpy, to be known and understood, must be made a subject of special study. The man who punctuates " by instinct " will make sorry work of it.

It seems strange that more attention has not been given to punctuation,—that it has not been considered important enough for a special text-book. There have been and are, in this country, the best of books on literary, historical, and all scientific subjects, save the important subject of punctuation. How has it come to pass that this necessary and interesting subject has been almost altogether overlooked? Doubtless it has been supposed that the few hints on the art, so briefly and tenderly given in some of the grammars, are sufficient.

The compiler of this little book, who has for a considerable time made punctuation a particular study, has not hesitated to make free use of such works on the subject as Quackenbos's, Allardyce's, Bigelow's and Wilson's. But the exercises, one or two excepted, have not been taken from any of the above works, but from every outside source that provided the best for illustrating the subject. Many have been taken from the School Readers ; and it is believed that they are sufficiently numerous and well-chosen to make a careful reader a fair pointer without any other aid. By inspecting a set of similarly punctuated sentences, one can easily recognize the principle common to each.

CONTENTS.

	PAGE
Preface,	5
The Comma,	9
The Semicolon,	30
The Colon,	33
The Period,	34
The Note of Interrogation,	35
The Note of Exclamation,	36
The Dash,	38
The Marks of Parenthesis	40
Brackets,	41
Quotation Marks,	42
The Apostrophe,	43
The Hyphen,	44
Other Marks,	44

A MANUAL OF PUNCTUATION.

CHAPTER I.—THE COMMA.

RULE I.

No mark is usually inserted between the subject and the predicate of a sentence.

Examples.

1. The first principle of narrative is to follow the order of events.

2. He who reads in a proper spirit can scarcely read too much.

3. But Master Johnny's serene confidence in his companion's seamanship was destined to be rudely shaken.

4. The difficulty of finding the little nests of the humming birds is increased by a curious habit possessed by some of the species.

(*a*) When the logical subject ends with a verb, and the predicate begins with a verb, a comma may be put between them; as, To say a thing is what it is, conveys no additional information.

(*b*) When the logical subject is long, and not easily seen as a whole, a comma may be placed after it; as, That some of the dissenting ministers were acquainted with Coppinger's intention, is plainly affirmed by himself.

(*c*) A comma is sometimes necessary to show whether a modifying word belongs to the subject or to the predicate; as, The boy that always does his work *quickly* advances to preferment. Here the sense will be determined by putting a comma after "work" or "quickly."

(*d*) When the nominative is followed by a pointed adjunct, a comma is required before the verb; as, The red sandstone rocks of Moray, Cromarty, and Ross, are covered by red-boulder clays.

(*e*) The case of two or more nominatives without a conjunction will be noticed under Rule IV.

RULE II.

When two words of the same part of speech are connected by *and* or *or*, no mark is inserted between them.

Examples.

1. Men and boys enjoy skating.
2. The bakers come and go.
3. The girls are quiet and attentive.
4. John or his brother will help us.
5. Never read hastily or carelessly.
6. I will go over or around the hill.

(*a*) But, should the first of two connected words be qualified by a term not applicable to the second, or the second be followed by a qualifying term not applicable to the first, a comma may be necessary before the conjunction; as, The children are *neatly* dressed, and provided with substantial food. He could draw, and paint fairly *well*.

(*b*) When the first of two phrases joined by a conjunction ends with a noun, and the second begins with a noun, a comma may precede the conjunction. And, when both have a common relation to the remainder of the sentence, a comma may be put after the last phrase; as, Refinement of mind, and clearness of thinking, usually result from grammatical studies.

(*c*) When *or* connects two words or expressions one of which explains the other, commas are used; as, Indian corn, or maize, flourishes in a warm climate.

RULE III.

When two words of the same part of speech, and in the same construction, are not joined by a conjunction, they are separated from each other by a comma.

THE COMMA.

Examples.

1. Follow the old, well-beaten path.
2. Eat, drink, what is on the table.
3. Moderate exercise of the body tones, strengthens it.
4. He was anxiously, momentarily expected.
5. Poor lone Hannah.
   Sitting at the window [,] binding shoes,
   Faded, wrinkled,
   Sitting, stitching, in a mournful muse.
6. Mistake, error, is the discipline through which we advance.
7. All lands, all seas, have heard we are brave.

(*a*) When the first of two adjectives qualifies the second and a noun, no mark is put between the adjectives ; as, The color of the tiger is a *light tawny* brown.

(*b*) When the first of two adverbs qualifies the second, no mark is put between them ; as, The boy acquitted himself *remarkably* well.

(*c*) When two prepositional phrases are joined together, having both prepositions expressed, a comma is generally put after the first phrase ; as, They married on a potato field, and at a cottier's rent. But, if the preposition is understood in the second phrase, no mark is used ; as, He was a man of sound judgment and great energy.

RULE IV.

Words of the same part of speech, in a series, are separated from each other by commas.

Examples.

1. The father, mother, and children were saved.
2. Wolfe, Moncton, and Murray landed with the 1st division.
3. Ages, countries, and individuals differ in their sense of what is excellent in composition.
4. Not a reptile, fish, mollusc, or zoophyte of the cretaceous system continues to live,

5. Cabbages, cherries, gooseberries, plums, apricots, and grapes might be now seen in English gardens.

6. The woman was poor, and old, and gray,
   And bent with the chill of the winter's day.

7. Collect, digest, and remember solid information.

8. This is what poses, perplexes, embarrasses, and torments you.

9. Julius Cæsar wrote in a clear, natural, correct, and flowing style.

10. This eminent man wrote purely, naturally, and perspicuously.

11. The savage is nature's thrall, whom she scorches, freezes, starves, drowns, as her caprice may dictate.

Every man, every horse, every dog, glorying in the plentitude (*sic*) of life is in a different attitude, motion, gesture, action.

Notice the first five examples. Some writers would omit the commas immediately before the conjunctions. But their insertion preserves the even connection or alternation between the particulars. Were the comma omitted before the conjunction in any one of these sentences, there would seem to be a stronger union or a greater alternation between the last two particulars than between the others, which is not the case. On the other hand, some would put a comma after the last particular. But it is altogether unnecessary, "because the conjunction shows," says Wilson, "that all the particulars have, either separately or together, a relation to what follows in the sentences."

(*a*) When the conjunction is omitted between the last two particulars of a series that makes the subject of a verb, a comma is put after the last particular; as, The earth, the air, the water, teem with delighted existence. Vituperation, abuse, depreciation, calumny, find a place in the oratory of all ages.

(*b*) When, in a series of verbs that have a common object, there is no conjunction between the last two, a comma follows the last verb; as, A teacher should not slight, discourage, ridicule, his pupils. If, however, the object be a monosyllable the comma may be omitted. See Example 3, Rule III.

(c). Words may be in juxtaposition, and not in a series; as, Early in the morning, men and boys go to work.

RULE V.

When words or expressions are used in apposition, they are set off by commas.

Examples.

1. Quebec, the Gibraltar of America, is on the St. Lawrence.
2. William Laud, Archbishop of Canterbury, directed the affairs of the church.
3. Prince Rupert, the nephew of Charles, led the Royalist cavalry.
4. In 1705, Thomas Newcomen, a smith and ironmonger, and John Crawley, a plumber and glazier, both of Dartmouth, in Devonshire, took out a patent for an improved machine, which they shared with Savery.

(a) When, however, a pronoun is added merely for emphasis, or when one of the words is used as a general name, the comma is omitted; as, I myself have seen it. Uncle George laughed heartily. The River St. Lawrence is the finest river in the world.

(b) When the parts of a compound names are given in order, no comma is used; as, John Campbell. But, when the order is inverted, the comma is used; as, Campbell, John.

(c) When a title is added to a proper name, it is set off by a comma; as, Rev. John Campbell, D.D. William H. Powers, Esq. Geo. F. Littlebone, LL.D., Buffalo, N.Y.

RULE VI.

Words repeated are separated by commas.

Examples.

1. Verily, verily, I say unto you.
2. No, no, Master Fox.
3. His effect of gravy, gravy, gravy.
4. Let me see, let me see. So, so, so, so : Yea, marry sir :—Ralph Mouldy! let them appear as I call; let them do so, let them do so.—Let me see; where is Mouldy?

RULE VII.

Words in pairs are separated into pairs by commas.

Examples.

1. Was he young or old, healthy or sickly, tractable or rebellious.
2. Earth to earth, ashes to ashes, dust to dust.
3. Upon his armory and his woodlands, his house and grounds, his furniture, and painting, he spent thousands of pounds.
4. Thus high and low are coupled, humble and suberb, momentous and trivial, common and extraordinary.
5. I have searched, I have enquired, so has my husband, man by man, boy by boy, servant by servant : the tithe of a hair was never lost in my house before.
6. And these have been corrected and recorrected, altered and revised, mended and re-mended, until we must have a very true and pure text of the poet in this century of ours.

RULE VIII.

When the members of a compound sentence need no pointing, they are, in animated discourse, often separated from one another by commas.

Examples.

1. The flesh of the bear is good to eat, and an oil is made of his fat.

2. Him they feared, him they trusted, him they obeyed.

3. Thus the child came to be an old man, and his face was wrinkled, and his steps were slow, and his back was bent.

4. A mania prevailed, a bubble burst, four stock brokers took villa residences at Florence, four hundred nobodies were ruined, and among them Mr. Nickleby.

RULE IX.

If adjective clauses or contracted adjective clauses are restrictive, no point is used ; but, if they are explanatory or parenthetical, they are marked off by commas.

Examples (Restrictive).

1. He that practises frugality becomes independent.
2. The pride that dines on vanity sups on contempt.
3. Everybody rushed out to see the horrible death they had escaped.
4. The meeting announced for Saturday night was postponed.
5. Among the most curious nests are those made by the birds called weavers.
6. This is a circumstance known to every one who has seen a file of ants on the march.

Examples (Parenthetical).

1. The juice, which looks much like dirty water, is heated in large iron or copper pans.
2. Not far from Cairo, which is now the principal city of Egypt, stand the famous pyramids.
3. The bodies are finally placed in huge stone coffins, many of which are covered with curious carvings.
4. My wife, who is an excellent rider, stuck close to me ; and my daughter, who was then a small child, I took in one arm.
5. One of these, named Damon, lived at some distance from Syracuse.

6. The "Emily St. Pierre" was a large Liverpool East India trader, commanded by Captain William Wilson.

By comparing an example of the first class with one of the second, a marked distinction between a restrictive and a parenthetical clause will be readily recognized. The first is *fastened* to its antecedent, and restricts it to a particular sense; and its attachment is so essential that without it the statement would be imperfect. The second is thrown in, or added as an independent explanation; and so loosely, that, were it omitted, the main statement would still be perfect. Quackenbos says: "The criterion is, will the meaning of the sentence be preserved if the expression be omitted? If so, it is parenthetical; if not, restrictive."

(*a*) If a word or clause, enclosed by commas, follow a restrictive relative, a comma may precede the relative, and especially if the antecedent be qualified by an adjective; as, It was only a few discerning friends, who, in the native vigor of his powers, perceived the dawn of Robertson's future eminence. "The reasons," says Wilson, "offered for this mode of punctuating are, that the adjective has some effect to loosen the restraining power of the relative over the antecedent; and that the omission of the comma between the two portions of such a sentence—between 'friends' and 'who' in the present example—would draw the pronoun more closely to the clause which precedes it, than to that of which it forms a part."

(*b*) When a restrictive pronoun has more than one antecedent, a comma should be put before it; as, As he passed through the busy, populous city of Seville, every window, balcony, and housetop, which could afford a glimpse of him, is described to have been crowded with spectators.

(*c*) "The practice of learning by rote strengthens the memory." "The man who makes the acquisition of money the sole object of his life is a sordid wretch." "There is no instance in modern history that equals it." In the first of these sentences, some writers would put a comma after "rote"; in the second, after "life"; and in the third, after "history." Such pointing, however, would not be well-considered work. The predicate of the first sentence can be satisfied with nothing less than "The practice of learning by rote." "Practice" cannot be separated from its adjunct. They are indissolubly united. Therefore, by Rule I., no comma is admissible. A similar consideration will suffice to show that no comma should be used after "life" in the second sentence. In the third sentence, the grammatical antecedent of "that" is "instance"; but "instance" cannot be separated "from in modern history." The real antecedent of "that" is "instance in modern history"; and, as "that equals it" restricts the antecedent, no comma can be put after "history."

Examples.

1. Happy is the man that findeth wisdom, and the man that getteth understanding.

2. The moderate tone of the work, which was written against the Puritans, is worthy of all praise.

3. Heat being [which is] motion, can be converted into mechanical force.

4. The little blacks on whom the red ants made this raid sallied out in considerable numbers; and I truly pitied them.

5. Soon after we came to a house, where [in which] we were kindly treated.

6. Lieutenant-Colonel G. T. Denison, who commands the body guard of the Governor-General of Canada, has brought out a "History of Cavalry."—*Westminster Review*.

7. The cipher written on his heaven-visited heart was deeper than his understanding could interpret.

8. The Hebrew is a very simple language, and hath not that variety either of moods or of conjunctions that is requisite for forming a complicated style.

9. Good instruction is a seed, which, sooner or later, will produce fruit.

10. Don't mind me, who, for the matter of years, might be your father or your uncle.

11. Each party, [whether it be] religious or political, scatters its sheets on all the winds.

12. On Blackheath stood Oliver's army, sad and angry, but conscious that they were no longer united.

RULE X.

A phrase, whether adjectival, participial or absolute, is separated from the remainder of the sentence by a comma; and, when it falls within a sentence, by a pair of commas.

Examples.

1. Quick to detect an error, he saw the mistake in a moment.

2. Baffled in three attempts to scale the wall, they could not be led to another assault.

3. Robert Brown, of Montrose, was a famous botanist.

4. Having caught some flakes on a piece of black cloth, Mr. Ray told the children to use the glass quickly.

5. Not willing to lose any of them, but unable to draw out his hand, he burst into tears.

6. Turning his cell and prison-yard into a little bower of sweet flowers, he lived there for two years, receiving visits from Byron, Moore, and other sympathetic friends.

7. The snow melts, the sun having risen.

8. The great object being thus effected, he departed for his home, being much easier in his mind.

9. The time of youth being precious, we should devote it to improvement.

10. To be plain, I do not understand you.

11. He is, all things considered, the safest guide on the river.

12. Taken all in all, it is one of the most delightful poems in our language.

(a) The absolute phrases, *to return, to proceed, to conclude, etc.*, when they begin a paragraph and refer to all of it, are generally followed by a colon.

RULE XI.

Adverbs and adverbial phrases, when they interrupt the flow of the discourse, are set off by commas.

Some of the adverbs and adverbial phrases so used are *also, too, then, however, perhaps, therefore, indeed, accordingly, meanwhile, likewise, moreover*, etc.; and *in short, no doubt, in truth, of course, for instance, to be brief, to be sure, generally speaking, at all events*, etc.

Examples.

1. Really, it is unbearable.
2. Well, you are a queer fish.
3. "Well, then, what is cotton?" inquired John.
4. "Yes, indeed," said the crow.
5. How weak I feel, to be sure.
6. By and by, up comes the round head of a seal.
7. He is, however, stingy in money matters, however generous he may be with advice.
8. He said, too, that the slate was too thin.
9. The sentinel, from time to time, paced near her.
10. In 1805, Nelson was killed at Trafalgar.
11. In some parts of Africa, no lady can be charming under twenty stone.
12. The bruise inflamed; and, after six weeks, the conqueror died near Rouen.
13. This, in effect, made his office hereditary; for, of course, he named his son.
14. Ovid, in one of his elegies, tells us that birds have a Paradise near Elysium. Doves, be sure, are not omitted.
15. In 1710, however, a strong force of four war vessels and nineteen transports, containing five regiments,

arrived at Port Royal, and, after a brave defence on the part of the besieged, took possession of the country.

16. Mr. James Watt, the great improver of the steam-engine, died on the 25th of August [,] 1819, at his seat of Heathfield, near Birmingham, in the eighty-fourth year of his age.

RULE XII.

Dependent clauses are usually separated by a comma from the rest of the sentence in which they occur, and always when intermediate.

Examples.

1. When the sun rose, the army stood upon the Plains of Abraham.
2. When they are roughly handled, they give out a strong aromatic smell.
3. Tell me about the plant, please.
4. Were such irregularities to prevail unchecked in our fleshy stores, we should suffer considerable annoyance.
5. Receiving him loyally, they offered to support him, if he would sign the Solemn·League.
6. Wherever I look or travel, in England or abroad, I see that men, wherever they can reach, destroy all beauty.
7. So, because I love odd names for little girls, I choose to call her Marygold.
8. Well, I believe I should have done so, if that meddlesome cook hadn't come in.
9. If a man of pleasure "about town" is swayed by anything, it is by a fear of becoming ridiculous.
10. Before I knew thee, Hal, I knew nothing; and now I am, if a man should speak truly, little better than one of the wicked.

(*a*) Wilson says: "When, in a sentence relating to time, place, or manner, the clause beginning with an adverb is put last, and is closely connected in sense with what precedes it, the comma should not be inserted ; as, 'I love my kind *where'er* I roam,' 'You will reap *as* you sow.' Clauses like these may be regarded as akin to the restrictive relative. But, if the adverbs *when*, *where*, etc., have only a faint reference to time or place, or introduce an additional idea, they should be preceded by a comma ; as, 'Refrain not to speak, *when* by speaking you may be useful to others,' 'Andrew sailed for California, where he does a flourishing business.'"

(*b*) We are face to face now with a point in punctuation on which the best authority and common sense are opposed to an extensive practice. Look at this sentence : "Come to-morrow ; and, if you can find your violin, bring it with you." Should there be a comma after "and," or not? Some put it there ; some do not. Wilson says : "Many writers are accustomed to omit the comma, in all cases, after a conjunction ; but it is evident, that, when a word of this or any other part of speech is divided by a phrase or clause from the portion of the sentence to which it belongs, such intervening expression should have a comma before as well as after it, as in the following example : 'Agamemnon still lives before us in the "tale of Troy divine" ; *but*, were not his name embalmed in that imperishable song, there would not now be a wreck of it.'" Quackenbos says : "Some are in the habit of omitting the comma before a parenthetical expression when it follows a conjunction. This is wrong ; there, as in every other position, it must be cut off by a comma on each side ; as, 'Your manners are affable, and, for the most part, pleasing.'" Mr. Allardyce says substantially the same, but seems to miss it sometimes in practice. He says : "But if the dependent clause be inserted parenthetically, it is marked off by commas or the other marks of parenthesis, however short it may be." This can hardly be called a typographical oversight ; it rather confirms a statement in his *Introduction*, that "few punctuate consistently," for the same carelessness can be found in other parts of his book. On page 27, there is, "But, where the connection between the adjective phrase and substantive is very close, and where there is no risk of ambiguity, no point is to be used." So far, so good. But, on page 17, he has, "But if they occur at the end of a sentence, another full stop is not added ; or, more correctly, it may be said that Rule IV. does not apply at the end of a sentence." And, on page 31, there is, "But where the words in apposition are used in a limiting or distinguishing sense, the principle of Rule XIV. applies, and no point is used. Thus we should write 'Burns, the poet,' 'Dickens, the novelist;' but, if we wished to distinguish them from another Burns and another Dickens, we should omit the comma." Mr. Bigelow has blemished a capital little book with this: "Where *but, and*, or other connecting particle, occurs after a period or semicolon immediately before a parenthetical clause, it is better to omit the comma before the parenthesis." This is a strange remark from a good man. If, as all punctuators agree, the prime object of punctuation is to show the structure of a sentence, so that the sense may be more readily perceived, it seems extraordinary that Mr. Bigelow would grant a license for such lop-sided work. Whenever a sentence is punctuated, it should be so done that its back-bone can be seen at a glance. Take this sentence.: "Albert Lee, *conscious in whose presence this eulogium was pronounced*, was much embarrassed ; but his father, *whose feelings were flattered by the panegyric*, was in rapture." And this : "The old man, *alive to the danger of his position*, called the aid of his son ; and, *when he arrived*, they soon despatched the bear." Although the main statements of these two sentences are made prominent, by throwing the subordinate parts into italics, yet the punctuation, without the italics, would make sufficiently plain the principal members of the sentences.

Examples.

1. But, if this were harsh, how would Mr. Gilfillan have had them proceed?

2. Yet, if we could forget Homer, we might not unreasonably be proud of it.

3. And, though we in English have abandoned the

artificial part of the system, we retain its fundamental distinction by our use of *he*, *she* and *it;* the test of sex is to us a real and ever-present one.

4. But, had his whole writings been of that same cast, he must have been degraded altogether, and a star would have fallen from our English galaxy of poets.

5. To make any beginning at all is one half the battle ; or, as a writer in this magazine suggests, a good deal more.

6. This was, however, put off from time to time ; and though I called often for it by appointment, I did not get it.

7. But the model of both poets was something different from the regular epic ; and if there must be a comparison, the standard is to be sought elsewhere.

8. A secret correspondence was held with France ; and, when all seemed ready, a day was fixed for the outbreak of rebellion.

9. But, when he was in Rome, he sought me out very diligently, and found me. 2 Tim. i. 17.

10. For even Christ pleased not himself ; but, as it is written, The reproaches of them that reproached thee fell on me. Rom. xv. 3.

(*c*) In Cooke's "New Chemistry," is this sentence : " Two bodies have the same temperature if, when placed together, neither of them gives or loses heat ; and, when, under the same conditions, one body loses while the other gains heat, that body which gives out heat is said to have the higher temperature." Here, a parenthetical phrase, " under the same conditions," is within a parenthetical clause, and has a comma at each end. But such pointing, however correct it may be considered, is altogether too stiff. Wilson says that short parenthetical expressions, " when introduced into what is itself parenthetical, should be left unpointed."

RULE XIII.

A short quotation, a maxim, or an important remark should be separated by a comma from the introductory clause.

Examples.

1. Said his sister's angel to the leader, "Is my brother come?" And he said, "Nay, but his maiden daughter."
2. Everybody knows the old saying, A stitch in time saves nine.
3. He ventured the bold assertion that rich men are seldom generous.
4. "The fact is, it ain't a hall," observed Squeers drily.
5. I say, it is a sin to give in to this system.
6. It is an old remark, that the most beautiful women are not always the most fascinating.

(*a*) If, however, the remark be preceded by a very short clause, the comma is not necessary; as, We know that the consequences will be serious. Accordingly, then, the comma in 5 should not be there; nor would it be, were the conjunction (*that*) used.

(*b*) Wilson says: "But if the remark or quotation consists of phrases which require to be punctuated, a comma should precede the conjunction [generally *that*], even when the introductory part of the sentence is quite short; as, '*Ossian says*, that sorrow, like a cloud on the sun, shaded the soul of Clessamour.' A comma should also be inserted after the conjunction, if an inverted or an adverbial phrase begins the remark; as, 'It is certain, *that*, in the declension of taste and science, language will degenerate.' The reason for the punctuation in such instances is, that the omission of the comma would bring the word 'that' into too close a contact with that part of the sentence with which it has the least affinity. For the sentence is obviously divisible into two portions, less connected than others which require to be pointed; the first ending, in the former of these examples, with the verb 'says,' and, in the latter, with the adjective 'certain.'

Mr. Bigelow says: "Clauses like 'It is said,' 'I answer,' 'He contended,' etc., introducing several propositions or quotations, each preceded by the word *that*, should have a comma before the first *that*, especially if the sentence is so constructed as to require a comma after the *that*."

Examples.

1. But it is evident, that, in respect to numerous other feelings, this statement does not hold good.

2. The expectation was, that, if captured, it would at once be sacked.

3. In like manner, it may be said of nonsense, that, in writing it, there is as great scope for variety of style as there is in writing sense.

4. It has been calculated by the ablest politicians, that no state, without being soon exhausted, can maintain above the hundredth part of its menbers in arms and idleness.

5. It cannot therefore follow, that, because a thing is true in the particular, it must be true in the universal.

6. It is to be observed, that, in her father's life, she had acknowledged his supremacy, and the justice of her mother's divorce.

7. The consolation was this, that, by the grace of God, up to that day not one of the congregation had been lost.

8. Remember ye not, that, when I was yet with you. I told you these things.—*2 Thess. ii. 5.*

9. Notwithstanding this, it will be found, that beginning with an easy transition from the Third Reader, the grading is gentle and regular throughout.

10. Two editions of Letters of Indulgence from Nicholas V., bearing the date of 1454, are extant in single printed sheets, and two more editions of 1455; but it has justly been observed, that, even if published before the Mazarin Bible, the printing of that great volume must have commenced long before.—*Hallam's Lit. of Europe, Chap. iii.*

RULE XIV.

All vocative words or expressions are separated by a comma from the rest of a sentence.

Examples.

1. Good day, boys.
2. Well, Froggie, you there still!
3. Are you hungry, old fellow?
4. Dear sir, When will you come to see me?
5. "What's to-day, my fine fellow?" said Scrooge.
6. How now, my sweet creature of bombast? How long is't ago, Jack, since thou sawest thine own knee?

RULE XV.

An ellipsis of a verb is generally indicated by a comma.

Examples.

1. The earlier portion of his career was devoted to fiction; the later portion, to his numerous historical and biographical sketches.
2. The settlements of wheat in Scotland extend to the north of Inverness; in Norway, to Drontheim; in Russia, to St. Petersburg.
3. Three lines drawn under a letter or word, in manuscript, show that it is to be printed in CAPITALS; two, in SMALL CAPITALS; one in *Italics*.
4. Haymakers got a penny a day; laborers, threehalfpence; carpenters, twopence; and masons, threepence.

(*a*) But, where there is no ambiguity without the comma, it is omitted; as, Thy state is taken for a jointstool, thy golden sceptre for a leaden dagger, and thy precious rich crown for a pitiful bald crown.

RULE XVI.

Transposed expressions are set off by commas.

Examples.

1. In his reasoning, Hobbes is admirably close and consistent.
2. What he could do, he seems to have done.

THE COMMA.

3. She was eight years old, she said.
4. There you are, you see.
5. You know Plornish, I think?
6. Among the original compositions in prose, is a large stock of Homilies, or Sermons.
7. What we profess to contemn, we scorn to refute.
8. To the natural gifts of a fine genius and a retentive memory, he added an indefatigable industry.

RULE XVII.

If two or more portions of a sentence have a common bearing on a succeeding clause or word, they are followed by commas.

Examples.

1. Rhetoric is the science, and oratory the art, of speaking well.
2. These incline to, and adopt, tenderness as a kindred quality.
3. Philosophy makes us wiser, Christianity makes us better, men.
4. Did not the priesthood, in the first ages, glory not in the name, but, what is better, in the office, of democrats.—*Alton Locke.*

Speaking of the practice dictated by this Rule, Wilson say, "And this, indeed, is the usage of the best, though perhaps not of the most numerous, punctuators."

RULE XVIII.

Contrasted words and phrases are separated by commas.

Examples.

1. There are many books in the world, but few good readers.
2. Consider yourself a free man, not a pensioner of anyone.

3. To buy cheap goods is not always true economy, but often a waste of means.

4. He possesses not only earnestness, but individuality and originality.

5. The greatest trouble is to be feared, not from the seditious speakers themselves, but from those who husband their anger in secret.

6. Though deep, yet clear ; though gentle, yet not dull ; strong, without rage ; without o'erflowing, full.

RULE XIX.

When a word or phrase that belongs to the first part of a sentence is tagged on to the end, a comma is generally necessary before the word or phrase.

Examples.

1. Add to your faith, virtue.
2. I brought all the sticks that it is made of, myself.
3. She is a very good girl, Amy.
4. I am a woman, I.
5. The book is very interesting, especially the first two chapters.
6. The word " wit " is said to be used, in Pope's Essay on Criticism, in *seven* different acceptations.
7. He saw the old crow perched on one of the branches, looking very grave.

RULE XX.

A comma is generally put before *that* when it means "in order to," before the infinitive of purpose, and especially when the infinitive is preceded by "in order."

Examples.

1. Shall we continue in sin, that grace may abound?
2. Sometimes it is necessary to sew two leaves together, that the space within may be large enough.

THE COMMA.

3. First, then, he sought out Breedge, to scold her heartily.

4. Newman jerked his head towards his little room, to signify that she was waiting there.

5. I am obliged to keep my wife continually at work helping me, in order to live.

6. Mr. Gallanbile dines late on the day of rest, in order to prevent the sinfulness of the cook's dressing herself.

RULE XXI.

Commas are used in full addresses, directions, referenees, etc.

Examples.

1. Whitby, December 25, 1890.
2. David Bushnell, grocer, 81, Highway, Pekin.
3. St. Matthew, xvii. 17. 1 Cor., ii. 12 : ix. 9.
4. *Handbook of Punctuation* and other *Typographical Matters.* By Marshall T. Bigelow, Corrector at the University Press, Cambridge, Mass. Price, 50 cents.
5. "Elements of Whistling." By John S. Harris, jun., 12mo, cloth, 50 cents. See Campbell's *Rhetoric*, pp. 21-24, 129-133, and 205.
6. "A Dream of the Gironde, and other Poems." By Evelyn Pyne. London : Smith, Elder, and Co., 1877.
7. The *Chicora* leaves Toronto at 2 o'clock, P.M., and returns at 7 in the evening.
8. The sun is 95,000,000 miles from the earth.

(*a*) The second example is pointed on the authority of Wilson. He says. " It is very usual, particularly in the United States, to omit the comma between the number of a house or shop and the street, and after the name of a month when preceding that of the year to which it belongs ; but, as these words are employed neither adjectively nor in apposition, the point should, beyond all doubt, be inserted ; as 'No. 140, Broadway, New York, January, 1855.'—' Thomas Tegg, bookseller, 73, Cheapside.' "

CHAPTER II.—THE SEMICOLON.

RULE I.

The semicolon is used to separate the clauses of a sentence, when the clauses themselves are subdivided by commas.

Examples.

1. In conduction, the bodies are in contact ; in radiation, they are some distance apart.
2. If they entered a house, he sat in the parlor ; if they peeped into the kitchen, he was there.
3.   Oft I had heard of Lucy Gray ;
        And, when I crossed the wild,
      I chanced to see at break of day
        The solitary child.
4. Napoleon, when he heard of this capitulation, was dismayed ; no incident, since the battle of Trafalgar, had affected him so much ; his ministers, alarmed at his depression, thought he had become suddenly indisposed.

RULE II.

The semicolon is used to separate short complete sentences, when the connexion between them is too close for periods.

Examples.

1. Another packet arrived ; she too was detained ; and, before we sailed, a fourth was expected.
2. Use no hurtful deceit ; think innocently and justly ; and, if you speak, speak accordingly.
3. The boy has turned to the right ; the man takes the left ; and the faster they both run, the farther they are asunder.
4. The wind and rain are over ; calm is the noon of day ; the clouds are divided in heaven ; over the green hills flies the inconstant sun.

THE SEMICOLON.

RULE III.

When a clause that expresses a reason or an explanation is appended to a perfect clause, the two clauses are separated by a semicolon.

Examples.

1. But even this is more ingenious than just ; for muttons, beeves, and porkers are good old words for the living quadrupeds.
2. And accordingly an able man may, by patient reasoning, attain any amount of mathematical truths ; because these are all implied in the definitions.
3. Make no expense but to do good to others or yourself ; that is, waste nothing.
4. But, taken as separate truths, viewed in the light of fragments and brilliant aphorisms, the majority of the passages have a mode of truth ; not of truth central and coherent, but of truth angular and splintered.

RULE IV.

The semicolon is used between expressions in a series that have a common dependence on an expression at the beginning, or the close, of a sentence.

Examples.

1. He said that he had been in the North-West ; that he had selected a homestead there ; and that he should go back in the autumn.
2. They returned with information, that the approach of that vast host was one of the most beautiful and terrible sights which could be seen ; that the whole country seemed covered with men-at-arms, on horse and foot ; that the number of standards, banners, and pennons [,] made so gallant a show, that the bravest and most numerous host in Christendom might be alarmed to see King Edward moving against them.
3. No day yet in the sky, but there was day in the resounding stones of the streets ; in the wagons, carts, and

coaches ; in the workers going to various occupations ; in the opening of early shops ; in the traffic at markets ; in the stir of the river side.

4. When we read of realms smitten with the scourge of famine or pestilence, or strewn with the bloody ashes of war ; of grass growing in the streets of great cities ; of ships rotting at the wharves ; of fathers burying their sons ; of strong men begging their bread ; of fields untilled ; and silent workshops, and despairing countenances,—we hear a voice of rebuke to our own clamorous sorrows and peevish complaints.

(*a*) But, if the clauses are short, commas are used ; as, May England never be ashamed to show to the world that she can love, that she can admire, that she can worship the greatest of her poets !

RULE V.

The semicolon is used also before *as, viz.; namely, to wit, that is, i.e.*, and *e.g.*, when examples are given, or subjects enumerated.

Examples.

1. The possessive pronoun never takes the apostrophe ; as, ours, yours, hers, theirs.

2. Names of places should always begin with capitals ; e.g., Buffalo, Rochester, Hamilton, Montreal.

3. Some men distinguish the period of the world into four ages ; viz., the golden age, the silver age, the brazen age and the iron age.

4. Maria Edgeworth's Works, 10 vols. Vol. I. Castle Rackrent ; An Essay on Irish Bulls ; An Essay on the Noble Science of Self-Justification ; Forrester ; The Prussian Vase ; The Good Aunt. Vol. II. Angelina ; The Good French Governess ; etc.

(*a*) When *as, namely, i.e.*, etc., are used parenthetically, they are preceded only by a comma ; as, In making these discriminations, another object has been kept in view, viz.; that of showing the *difference of usage*, in respect to certain words, between the United States and England.

THE COLON.

RULE I.

The colon is sometimes used to separate two short sentences which are too closely connected to be set off into periods, but too weakly connected to be divided by a semicolon.

Examples.

1. Be on your guard against flattery: it is an insidious poison.
2. He walked deliberately into the room: no one dared oppose him.

RULE II.

The colon may be used to separate clauses that are subdivided by semicolons.

Examples.

1. For now we see through a glass darkly; but then face to face: now I know in part; but then shall I know even as also I am known.
2. Vainly we offer each ample oblation;
    Vainly with gifts would his favor secure:
    Richer by far is the heart's adoration;
    Dearer to God are the prayers of the poor.

RULE III.

The colon is put before a long quotation, and sometimes before a specification of particulars which are not formally introduced, and especially so if the particulars are pointed by semicolons.

Examples.

1. But, after a long pause, he said : "Although I am no advocate of this man's cause," etc.
2. In the first place, it sets aside and denies two other conceivable answers : that language is a race characteristic, and, as such, inherited from one's ancestry, along with color, physical constitution, traits of character, and the like : and that it is independently produced by each individual, in the natural course of his bodily and mental growth.

(*a*) When the quotation begins a new paragraph, a dash follows the colon.

RULE IV.

The colon is used on title pages, between the place of publication and the publisher's name.

Examples.

1. Toronto : Educational Publishing Co.
2. New York : Appleton & Co.
3. London : Macmillan & Co.

THE PERIOD.

The period, or full point, is used at the end of every sentence that is neither exclamatory nor interrogative.

It is used after a heading or a sub-heading ; after the address of a letter, and after a signature ; and after the name and description of a book, before the author's name on a title page.

It is put after every abbreviated word, and after Roman numerals, and sometimes between Roman numerals, to facilitate the reading of them.

Periods are also used to denote an omission in a quotation. If part of a sentence be omitted, three periods are used ; if a complete sentence be left out, four periods are used ; but, if a paragraph be left out, a line of five or six periods is generally used.

The period is also employed for leaders in tabular work, to carry the reader's eye to the proper place ; and before decimals, and between pounds and shillings and pence.

THE NOTE OF INTERROGATION.

RULE I.

The interrogation point is put after a direct question.

1. What are those queer-looking things yonder?
2. And how if I refuse to shoot on such a wager?
3. You will stop for supper?
4. Have you ever used the expression, "plain as a pikestaff"?

RULE II.

When a sentence contains more than one question, and each question requires a distinct answer, the point of interrogation is put after each question ; but, if one answer suffices for all the questions, one note of interrogation is put at the end.

Examples.

1. Where are you going?—to Bristol, to Bath, to Plymouth, or to Falmouth?
2. Wherein is he good, but to taste sack and drink it? wherein neat and cleanly, but to carve a capon and eat it? wherein cunning, but in craft? wherein crafty, but in villany; wherein villainous, but in all things? wherein worthy, but in nothing?
3. Do you fancy that you can again deceive me, cheat me, and hold me up to ridicule?
4. Ah! whither now are fled those dreams of greatness, those busy, bustling days, those gay-spent, festive nights,

those veering thoughts, lost between good and ill, that shared thy life?

(*a*) When in a quotation an expression occurs, that is doubtful or merits a denial, the transcriber sometimes puts after it, in brackets, a note of interrogation; as, "The Captain fed the crew on fresh beef [?] during the whole voyage."

THE NOTE OF EXCLAMATION.

RULE I.

The note of exclamation is used after interjections, and sentences expressing wonder, a wish, or surprise.

Examples.

1. Ah! So you have made a discovery since yesterday?

2. "Very miserable! indeed!" exclaimed the stranger; "and how happens that?"

3. Give you a reason on compulsion! if reasons were as plenty as blackberries, I would give no man a reason upon compulsiou, I.

4. Stop, thief! stop, thief!—a highwayman!

5. May Shakespeare live on in the love of each generation that grows up in England!

6. Now let me point out, and show you what wonders *chance* can do!

(*a*) Between *O* and *Oh*, there is a difference. The first is properly used in a direct address, but the latter is never so used. Immediately after *O*, the note of exclamation should not be put; but, if it begins a sentence that is highly passionate or exclamatory, a note of exclamation may close the sentence. After *Oh*, the mark is immediately placed, although, when the sentence requires at its close the same mark, the note may be omitted after *Oh*,

THE NOTE OF EXCLAMATION.

Examples.

1. O my child, my dear child !
2. Mother, O mother, my heart calls for you.
3. O Hal, I prithee, give me leave to breathe awhile.
4. Oh ! I'm the chief of Ulva's Isle.
5. Oh ! what is man, when at ambition's height ?
6. Oh ! ancient fisherman, go up to yonder cot !

(*b*). When a sentence is interrogative in form, but exclamatory in force, the note of exclamation is put after it ; as, " How could he have been so foolish ! "

CHAPTER III.—THE DASH.

RULE I.

The dash is used when the subject is abruptly changed; when the sense is for a moment suspended, and then continued; and where a pause is required.

Examples.

1. As I said before, he refused to tell me—Who is knocking?
2. Sir John stands to his word—the devil shall have his bargain; for he was never yet a breaker of proverbs—he will give the devil his due.
3. Where hast thou been?—what hast thou seen?—what strange uncertainty is in thy looks?—and why dost thou not answer me?
4. He shook his head;—he sat down in despair;—he ran round in a circle;—he dashed into the woods and back again.

RULE II.

The dash is used to indicate a faltering speech.

Examples.

1. Yes—that is—you know what I mean?
2. He undertook to make an explanation; but—the—it was seen—his brother silenced him.

RULE III.

When a parenthetical clause is too closely related to the whole sentence to be put in parentheses, but yet needs some stronger marks than commas, to separate it from the other parts of the sentence, a dash may be put before and after it. And, if it be inserted where there is a comma, a comma must be placed before each dash.

THE DASH.

Examples.

1. The fish-otter—which is found around lakes and rivers in Canada, in the United States, in South America, and in wild parts of Europe—is a famous fisher.

2. According to many writers,—according to Ricardo himself and Mr. M'Culloch,—the answer was occasionally not amiss; only it was unsteady and vacillating.

RULE IV.

When several subjects that constitute a nominative are broken off and resumed in a new form, or when a series of expressions lead to an important conclusion, the dash is used.

Examples.

1. Invention, fabrication, devisal, production, generation,—all these are terms which have their favorers and also their violent opposers.

2. The lamp burning dimly in the socket, the wood fire almost extinguished in its own white embers, the gloomy picture over the chimney piece, the sealed packet on the table,—all reminded him of the events of yesterday, and his deliberations of the succeeding night.

RULE V.

When, in a specification of particulars, there is an ellipsis of *that is*, *namely*, and such words, the dash preceded by a comma is properly used. The comma indicates the apposition; the dash, the pause. (Cf. Colon, Rule III.)

Examples.

1. Gilliatt had but one resource,—his knife.

2. Do you know the pods of the honey-locust trees,—large, broad, thin, and sweet?

3. In speaking there are three principal ends,—to inform, to persuade, to please.

4. There he paused, not knowing which way to turn; for two paths were before him,—one to the right and one to the left.

RULE VI.

The dash is used between the side heading of a paragraph and the paragraph; after a quotation, before the author's name; and in rhetorical repetition.

Examples.

1. ORDER.—Let all your things have their places; let each part of your business have its time.
2. "If all the year were playing holidays,
   To sport would be as tedious as to work."
   —*Shakespeare.*
3. Cannot you, with your ability—cannot you, without any difficulty—cannot you do it for me?

(*a*) The dash denotes an omission; as, Mr. H——d has gone to R——r.

THE MARKS OF PARENTHESIS.

The marks of parenthesis are used to enclose words that break the unity of a sentence; they enclose matter that does not strictly belong to the sentence. When a parenthesis is inserted in a sentence where there is no comma, no point is used before or after either parenthesis. If it be inserted where there is a comma, and the included remark relate to something before it, a comma is put after the last parenthesis; but, if the remark relate to the whole sentence, a comma is put before each parenthesis.

Examples.

1. What the French King chiefly relied upon (besides his great numbers) was the troop of fifteen thousand cross-bowmen from Genoa.

2. He lifted the door-latch (it was brass only a moment ago, but golden when his fingers quitted it), and emerged into the garden.

3. Know then this truth, (enough for man to know,) Virtue is happiness below.

4. A young officer (in what army, no matter) had so far forgotten himself, in a moment of irritation, as to strike a private soldier, full of personal dignity, (as sometimes happens in all ranks,) and distinguished for his courage.

(*a*) A parenthesis sometimes constitutes an independent sentence, and, when it does so, the closing mark—period, note of interrogation, or note of exclamation—is put before the last parenthesis; as, (He seemed quite indifferent while I told him all this.) This is neater than putting the period after the last parenthesis, as is sometimes done.

(*b*) Parentheses are often used where commas would be more suitable.

BRACKETS.

Brackets are used for explanations thrown into a quotation by the transcriber; if he introduces a correction or a short note, he puts *his* remark in brackets. By doing so, his remarks can be distinguished from the author's, who may have used parentheses in the very passage quoted.

Examples.

1. A fleet of twenty ships were [was] in the bay.

2. *Verner.* [Rushing forward.] Here, Tell.

3. "She [the poor little match girl] was frozen to death, and a bundle of burnt matches lay beside her."

4. Yawning most volcanically, he made up to one of the room windows, were (*sic*) stood a large water-bottle or jar, one of those long-necked clay things in which they usually keep fluids in the East.

(*a*) In the last example, *sic* is put after "were," to show that the quotation is faithfully given ; and *this word* is generally inserted in parentheses. But in actual work it would be mere trifling to copy a clerical error so palpable. It is done here, as in Ex. 12, Rule IV. of the Comma, to exemplify the use of *sic*.

QUOTATION MARKS.

Marks of Quotation [" "], which consist of two inverted commas and two apostrophes, are used to indicate a passage taken from another writer, or to mark a repetition of what a writer himself had already said.

When a quotation is within a quotation, the included one is indicated by single marks, and, if another be inserted into the second, the double marks are again used.

A phrase or a saying from a foreign language is usually put in italics.

When an extract consists of successive paragraphs, each paragraph begins with inverted commas, but the apostrophes are not used until the final close. It was customary to prefix inverted commas at the beginning of every line of a quotation, but it is seldom done now.

Names of books, ships, etc., are correctly put in quotation marks, though for neatness they are often put in italics.

Examples.

1. Lamb says, " Why are we never quite at our ease in the presence of a schoolmaster?—because we are couscious that he is not quite at ease in ours."

2. In the "Third Reader," are these two sentences: "The innkeeper begged him not to proceed. 'There is danger ahead,' said he: 'the wolves are out.'"

3. With him, *Stat pro ratione voluntas.*

4. In Franklin's "Autobiography," are the following paragraphs :—

"William Maugridge, joiner, but a most exquisite mechanic, and a solid, sensible man.

"Hugh Meredith, Stephen Potts, and George Webb, I have characterized before.

"Robert Grace, a young gentleman of some fortune, generous, lively, and witty; a lover of punning and of his friends."

5. Last winter I read Smith's "Wealth of Nations," Whitney's "Life and Growth of Language," and several articles in Appleton's "Encyclopedia;" but lately I have consumed my leisure with the *Edinburgh Review*, the *Atlantic Monthly*, *Blackwood*, and some lighter reading.

6. Three frigates were in the harbour,—the *Shannon*, *Arethusa*, and the *Clio*.

(a) " are called *The Turn*;" are called *The Close*.

THE APOSTROPHE.

RULE I.

The apostrophe is used to denote the elision of a letter or letters.

Examples.

I've, for *I have*; *he's*, for *he is*; *you'll*, for *you will*; *'tis*, for *it is*; *don't*, for *do not*; *ne'er*, for *never*; *o'er*, for *over*; etc.

(a) It is also used to denote the omission of figures; as, The rough old times of '59 (1859).—It happened during the years, 1861, '62, '63, '64, and '65.

(b) It is inserted to aid in forming the plural of letters and figures; as, Cross your *t's* and dot your *i's*.—Make your *5's* and *8's* plainer.—In our village there are no less than four M.D.'s.

RULE II.

The apostrophe is used to mark the possessive case.

Examples.

John's Book.—The boys' yard.—Nicholas's hat.—Dickens's novels.—Burns's poems.

THE HYPHEN.

The hyphen is used between compound words that together would not be recognized as a single word ; it is also used between a prefix ending in a vowel and a word beginning with the same vowel, to show that each of the vowels must have a separate pronunciation ; and to mark a break in a word at the end of a line.

Examples.

1. Glass-house, night-time, half-dollar, twenty-third, one-horse concern, crow's-nest, vice-president, etc.

2. Pre-existence, re-examine, re-echo, co-operate, co-ordinate, etc.

(*a*) When an expression is used as a qualifying epithet, the words forming the expression may be connected by hyphens ; as, It is some out-of-the-world place.

(*b*) In dictionaries the hyphen is used between the syllables of words, to aid in the pronunciation.

OTHER MARKS.

Two Commas.—Two inverted commas are often used to save the repetition of a word that is common to several cases ; as,—

James Booth......................Toronto.
James Welsh......................   "

OTHER MARKS. 4

The Caret.—The caret is used to show the omission of a letter or a word ; as,—

        l   may
Some vilage Hampden here rest.
        ^   ^

The Index.—The index, or hand, calls for special attention to a remark ; as, ☞ *All arrears must be settled at once.*

Marks of Ellipsis.—Ellipsis is indicated in three ways. —by means of a long dash, a series of periods, or of stars; as, C——s is very clever.—The book . . . is very old.—In California, he worked very hard. * * * * But, when he came home, he was still poor.

Leaders.—Leader are dots, used mostly in tabular work, to lead the eye to the end of a line ; as

    John Watts........................Room 63
    James Holt........................ "   21

Reference Marks.—The Asterisk [*], the Dagger [†], the Double Dagger [‡], the Section [§], the Parallel Lines [‖], and the Paragraph [¶] are used "when references are made to observations or notes in the margin."

Supplementary Exercises

FOR FIRST CLASSES:
    Drill Arithmetic, 10c.; teachers' edition, 15c.
    Exercises in Arithmetic (teachers only), 15c.
    Phonics, Vocal Expressions and Spelling, 25c.
    Mental Arithmetic Exercises, Part I., 10c.
    Junior Language Lessons, 10c.

FOR SECOND CLASSES:
    Drill Arithmetic, 10c.; teachers' edition, 15c.
    Junior Language Lessons, 10c.
    Exercises in Arithmetic, 10c.; teachers' edition with answers, 15c.
    Mental Arithmetic Exercises, Part I., 10c.

FOR THIRD CLASSES:
    Canadian History Notes, 10c.
    Geography Notes, 10c.
    Junior Language Lessons, 10c.
    Exercises in Grammar, 10c.
    How We are Governed, 10c.
    Mental Arithmetic Exercises, Part I., 10c.
    Exercises in Arithmetic for Third Classes, 10c.; teachers' edition with answers, 15c.
    Drill Arithmetic, 10c.; teachers' edition, 15c.
    Summary of Canadian History in Verse, 5c
    Map of Canals, 10c.

Supplementary Exercises

FOR FOURTH CLASSES :
    Canadian History Notes, 10c.
    British History Notes, 10c.
    Geography Notes, 10c.
    Physiology and Hygiene Notes, 10c.
    Exercises in Composition, 10c.
    Exercises in Grammar, 10c.
    How We are Governed, 10c.
    Mental Arithmetic Exercises, Part II., 10c.
    Exercises in Arithmetic, 10c ; teachers' edition with answers, 15c.
    Drill Arithmetic, 10c.; teachers' edition, 15c.
    Summary of Canadian History in Verse, 5c.
    Manual of Punctuation, 10c.
    Entrance Examination Papers for the Past Five Years, 10c.; or in lots of two or more, 7c.
    Map of Canals, 10c.

FOR FIFTH CLASSES :
    Canadian History Notes, 10c.
    British History Notes, 10c.
    British History in Brief, 30c.
    Astronomical and Mathematical Geography, 25c.
    Hard Places in Grammar Made Easy, 20c.
    Geography Notes, 10c.
    Exercises in Arithmetic, 10c. teachers' edition containing answers, 15c.
    Mental Arithmetic Exercises, Part II., 10c.
    Drill Arithmetic, 10c.: teachers' edition, 15c.
    Exercises in Composition, 10c.
    How We are Governed, 10c.
    Manual of Punctuation, 10c
    Map of Canals, 10c.